Family Walks in
Northern Lakeland

by
Bob Swallow

GW00726055

DALESMAN

First Published in Great Britain 1993 by
Dalesman Publishing Company Limited,
Stable Courtyard, Broughton Hall,
Skipton, North Yorkshire BD23 3AE
Text and drawings © 1993 **Bob Swallow**

For Stan and Freda

ISBN **1 85568 062 9**
Typeset by **Lands Services, East Molesey, Surrey.**
Printed by **Lavenham Press, Lavenham, Suffolk.**

Contents

INTRODUCTION

FOLLOWING my earlier book, *Family Walks in Central Lakeland*, (Dalesman 1991) my boots have gravitated north west. This is an area close to my heart and effectively where I came in back in 1963.

My wife Pauline and I had married that February and in the autumn stole a long weekend in the Dales and Lakes. On an appalling November evening we descended Newlands in our battered Austin A35. The wipers were only about six inches long and totally inadequate to contend with the deluge. A wildly swinging sign offered B and B and, after a thirteen point turn we eventually negotiated the acute corner and steep descent to Gillbrow Farm. May Wilson was sorry there was not much to eat. An hour later we were not, sitting there fit to bust beside a roaring fire. So was a love affair born.

There on the shelf, freshly published, was a copy of A. Wainright's *North Western Fells*. You would have thought Ike Wilson the farmer would have known each fell intimately. Not so. He knew and doubtless still does every stone on Robinson, home to 400 head of sheep. Catbells on the other hand might well be on foreign territory. The farm is now largely run by son John, Ike and May having moved all of 15 yards to the delightful converted barn next door.

Newlands, you will gather, holds special affection for me but so too does north west Lakeland in general. To really appreciate the area try to avoid bank holidays plus July and August. The scenery is better in any other season bar summer. Glorious autumn tints, crystal clear days in winter and the fresh joy of spring. Beyond Newlands Hause the Buttermere Valley offers more attractions, all scenic, not a juke box in sight. Loweswater is a special haven for lovers of peace and quiet, please respect it.

My old pals Bill, Colin and Stan all figure again in these pages, indeed this is now Stan's home patch, lucky beggar.

The walks are suitable for all ages, the most strenuous being Styhead and Sprinkling Tarn. They vary in length from 2½ to 8½ miles and are all to be found on the 1:25000 ordnance map of the English Lakes, North West Sheet. Let me quickly qualify that statement before I am pulled up. All bar ½ mile of the area around Sprinkling Tarn on Walk No. 5. 1:25000 equates to 2½ inches to the mile if, like me, your are non-metric. For that reason all units of measure in this book are imperial. If it helps, one foot equals 0.3048 metres and one mile 1.6090 kilometres, this in special deference to Euro walkers.

On this occasion I have decided to include a grid reference as one or two starting points are a little off the main tourist tracks.

There is still an aura of mystique surrounding grid references, not to mention compass bearings. By all means take a compass if it makes you feel better, on these walks you should not need it. Grid references are however extremely useful. The trick is in knowing how to read them. There is an example shown on the ordnance sheet yet folk still get mixed up as to where to start. The map is crossed by two sets of lines, vertical and horizontal dividing the whole into squares. Remember the phrase, "Evening comes before the night". Bearing that in mind look for Fangs Brow, Walk No. 8 grid ref. 106226. Work east (evening) from the bottom left corner of the map to find the vertical line 10. Now follow this north (night) until meeting the horizontal line 22. So far you have located 10_22_. The two missing digits are estimates respectively east 6/10ths and north 6/10ths again making up the whole reference. Easy.

Boots are requested for your own comfort, there being no fun in having wet feet for half a day unless of course you are a youngster hell bent on getting soaked through. I have met on my travels a few folk at the opposite end of the age spectrum who appear to be going through a second childhood in this respect. Most people will, however, benefit from decent footwear.

On that note let me close by once more reminding you of Alfred Wainright's exhortation to, "Watch where you are putting your feet".

Lines to Latrigg

Start and Finish: The Moot Hall, Keswick grid ref. 267234. An easy early section following the course of the erstwhile Cockermouth, Keswick and Penrith Railway from Keswick through the Greta Gorge to Threlkeld. Return is by field paths and tracks over the airy summit of Latrigg, a viewpoint unsurpassed for Derwentwater and the Jaws of Borrowdale.
Distance: 8½ miles. (7½ by direct descent of Latrigg.)
Climbing: 1000 feet.
Time: 5 hours.
Map: O.S. English Lakes 1:25000 North West.
Public Transport: Keswick Bus Station is well served by routes from Kendal and the south; West Cumbria; Carlisle; Wigton and Penrith.

Start:
FROM the Moot Hall in the centre of Keswick walk in the direction of the bus station to the left of the main street. Opposite lies Stanger Street pointing towards Skiddaw. Climb to the brow of this hilly cul-de-sac, noting the excellent retrospective view over the rooftops to Catbells and Borrowdale.

Dipping towards the River Greta, bear right then cross the footbridge into Fitz Park. Skirt the edge of the cricket ground passing behind the pavilion and children's play area before climbing steps to Station Road adjacent the Keswick Art Gallery and museum which is incidentally well worth a visit.

Go to the right of Keswick Spa swimming pool to gain the trackbed of the old railway alongside what was formerly platform 1. The Cockermouth, Keswick and Penrith Railway (C.K.P.R.) with its link to Workington was originally conceived primarily to transport pig iron from West Cumberland to the North East. Coal was carried in the reverse direction. A passenger service was inaugurated within two months of the line opening in November 1864, being retained until its eventual demise in 1972.

Keswick station in its heyday was a busy spot boasting three platform faces. There was a covered way linking the station with The Keswick Hotel. During the Second World War, Roedean School was removed lock, stock and barrel to Keswick from the vulnerable south coast. Many of the station rooms became classrooms, it even being recorded that dances were staged on the island platform.

Platform 1 has now had its glass roof and buildings refurbished as part of the Keswick Spa complex, even down to lookalike station signs. From the throat of the station a pedestrian way has been provided, the original ballast – hard on the feet – topped with water gravel to make a more even surface. A bridge is crossed, the road beneath leading to Brundholme Woods, followed almost immediately by another, this time on the skew over the River Greta and the road bound for Ambleside. This, the first of many river crossings east of Keswick made the C.K.P.R. an extremely expensive stretch of line to both build and maintain.

An embankment follows looking down on the back of long-gardened semis. Ducking beneath a bridge the trackbed appears to shoot uphill at an alarming gradient. The land here has been "made" on the approach to the comparatively modern bridge spanning the Greta at Brigham Forge and carrying the A66 bypass to the north of Keswick. This bridge I always refer to as "Europa" after its continental big brother, its setting being similarly dramatic.

Pass beneath the bridge, the path beyond climbing to road level before dropping steeply over the eastern mouth of the erstwhile "Big Tunnel", its western portal lost under the infilling just traversed.

A most spectacular section follows, the trackbed initially buttressed to a rockface with the river flowing way below, a weir feeding a former mill race. The track maintains a relatively straight course whilst the river takes the easiest line being thus crossed and recrossed by a series of overstrung and understrung bow girder bridges, some on the skew. The route was difficult to work, continuing as it did over Stainmoor, at that time the highest railway in the country. Many years ago I brought my wife and young family up this stretch. The decking on many bridges was missing, it being necessary to cross on the huge wooden beams to which the track had been bolted. The kids loved it, though Pauline was none too keen on the swirling torrent thirty feet below with little – if any – protection. Happily, the Lake District Special Planning Board have undertaken to maintain a footpath over the section to Threlkeld so long as the bridges remain safe for pedestrians. Congratulations to them on their enterprise.

In fact there is now provision to take wheelchairs on the track-bed from a short platform still in situ at Briery Bobbin Mill which only closed in 1958 when work ceased at the mill. A notice here gives a wealth of information including the fact that at the height of production 400 million bobbins were being produced annually which, if placed end to end, would have stretched 800 miles. There was a siding here serving the mill where now stand static caravans.

The woods encroaching the lineside are a joy to behold, the last two weeks in October on the right day being at their most spec-tacular. A minor lane drops within a few yards of the old railway where Glenderraterra Beck meets the river Glenderramackin to

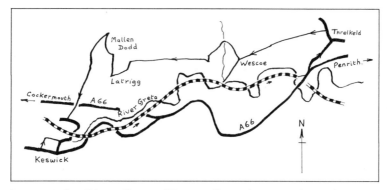

become the River Greta. Here a line of escape is available if flagging, allowing a walk back through the woods on the lower slopes of Latrigg. Also at this point is a former lengthsman's cabin, re-roofed and seated, part of a wall removed to provide an excellent prospect of Blencathra building up to the east. A wealth of information on wildlife is available including also that the average flow of the Greta at this point is equivalent to 100 full tankers passing every minute or 1000 such vehicles when in spate.

As Stan and I sat having a cuppa one recent August day at this four star butty stop, a pair of swallows screamed by outside, until one in a bold move shot in to alight momentarily atop the old flue pipe. Three beaks opened as one, amid considerable noise. We sat for half an hour observing feeding time.

Beyond in an almost Alpine setting, having crossed one bridge, the short Wescoe Wood Tunnel is entered on a curve followed by another bridge this time on the skew as the river loops back. This must have been a rare place to view the northern portion of The Lakes Express climbing wearily up the grade, possibly an Ivatt Class 2 or even a pair at its head. Threequarters of a mile on, beyond another butty cabin a path leads steeply to the A66 Threlkeld bypass. Turn left within yards at the sign for Threlkeld. Traffic on the village lanes is light. In the centre, a further sign points up tarmac to Blencathra. Ignore the track immediately on your right, continuing upward, passing the school before taking to a footpath at Town Head Farm marked Wescoe and Keswick. When faced by a pair of gates opt for the left thereafter negotiating a series of stiles to eventually emerge at Wescoe after passing a renovated property with notices requesting you to "Shut that gate – use Coopers Dip". Try not to blunder about too much in this area, Stan and I being past masters of the art have some excuse, waymarking has however of recent years improved over this section and there should be no difficulty.

At the hamlet of Wescoe there is a choice of lanes, that to the left returning to the outward route at the confluence of Glenderraterra and Glenderramackin. Go right noting a post box set in the barn wall. Soon the track is met descending from England's loneliest property, Skiddaw House, set in the heart of Skiddaw Forest where paradoxically the few remaining trees stand as windbreaks around the row of former shepherd's cottages which trade as Skiddaw House.

Remember the Herries Chronicles by Hugh Walpole? Skiddaw House being the place where Uhland and John had their final showdown on a day when the mist writhed its way down the fell-sides with all the venom of a bagful of vipers. It still sends a shiver down my spine when I visit the place even on a good day.

Follow tarmac left to Derwentfolds before descending a rough track to the Glenderraterra, here set deep in woodland. Cross the narrow bridge to climb the opposite slope joining a lane leading right to a mini col. Pause to take in the view at a convenient gate. Left to right. High Rigg; Raven Crag; Shouthwaite Gill; Bleaberry Fell; Walla Crag; High Spy; Maiden Moor; Hindscarth; Cat Bells; Robinson; Red Pike Ridge and Causey Pike. Oh and yes, Latrigg.

At the col and through another gate starts the path to Skiddaw, climbing steadily. Beyond a gate where conifers start on the right, ascend the fellside – no track – to a curious rake following the contour to a fence corner. A path materialises by this fence but soon a stile is found leading unerringly to the summit of Latrigg. The walk is recommended in this direction to take full advantage of this excellent viewpoint, the full extent of which is not apparent until gaining the highest point. Beneath your feet lies Keswick clustered round the shores of Derwentwater, this in turn leading the eye to the Jaws of Borrowdale.

Here is a spot to sit and linger, definitely a major butty stop. Latrigg caters even for the elderly, the Gale Road terminating within ⅓ mile and 230 feet of its modest 1203 feet to which there is easy access over velvety turf. It is also an excellent place to watch the sunset during early spring or mid autumn – paradise before you.

Return to Keswick is easy, either proceeding straight ahead to an unremitting steep descent to Spooney Green Lane towards which children will bowl at speed, or in more sedate fashion via clear easy path zig-zagging around Mallen Dodd to meet the direct route below Whinney Brow. Spooney Green Lane is the name of this delightful lower stretch crossing the bypass to join a quiet road to the rear of the old station site, much of which is covered by housing. Bear left, then right, under the station bridge into Station Road recrossing the Greta and return to the Moot Hall to conclude a walk of great beauty and variety which calls me back time and again.

Friar's Crag and Castlehead Wood

Start and Finish: The Moot Hall, Keswick. Grid ref. 267234. A very easy walk eminently suited to afternoon arrival at the start of a week's holiday. Visiting a popular beauty spot and an excellent viewpoint both with a minimum of effort. Ideal for newcomers to the area.
Distance: 2½ miles.
Climbing: 150 feet.
Time: 1½ hours.
Map: English Lakes: 1:25000 North West.
Public Transport: Keswick bus station is well served by routes from Kendal and the south; West Cumbria; Carlisle; Wigton and Penrith.

Start:
FROM the Moot Hall and facing Woolworths walk left past Barclays Bank and a variety of shops until, framed by a fine beech, the legendary George Fisher's walking and climbing emporium comes into view. Turn right down Lake Road passing through the subway to emerge at The Heads, a crescent of large properties now almost exclusively offering tourist accommodation.

Hope Park is ahead, donated in 1974 by Sir Percy and Lady Hope to the town for the benefit of both residents and visitors. There are several commemorative seats. A mini golf course is well patronised. Leave the park at the far end. Opposite lies one of Keswicks prime attractions, the famous Blue Box (Century) Theatre. Literally a series of boxes on wheels, the contraption toured the country for many years before finally coming to rest in Keswick, its joints and moving parts worn out. Its immobility has been the town's gain. Aesthetically it offers little but the pleasure it has provided to countless thousands is beyond price. Now its days are numbered, a replacement theatre to be built near Keswick Spa. It will be a sad day when the discerning theatregoer no longer has to don cagoul when seated under certain roof joints on a wet night. Personally, I shall always associate "The Blue Box" with Derek Forss and his superb audio visual productions of the district.

Turn right detouring into Crow Park for a view down the lake. On the right is the sea-serpent-like summit of Causey Pike and, further around, Grisedale Pike. Between the two lies the mid height of Barrow. Newlands Valley is seen to good effect, on its left Hawse End leading upward to the lowly yet dramatic peak of Cat Bells stretching beyond to Maiden Moor and High Spy.

In the foreground is Derwent Isle, Keswick Launch landing to its left. The launches are an invaluable means of transport for Borrowdale calling at several points around the lake.

Retrace your steps now to the boat landings, following tarmac past picnic tables flanked on the left by Cockshot Wood, mainly beech and sessile oak. Over a hawthorn hedge may be seen the rugged face of Walla Crag, Great Wood extending upward to within 100 feet of its summit.

The National Trust emblem is found at the approach to Friar's Crag, followed shortly by the memorial to Canon Hardwicke Drummond Rawnsley 1851-1920, Canon of Carlisle; Chaplain to the King and one of the founders of the National Trust.

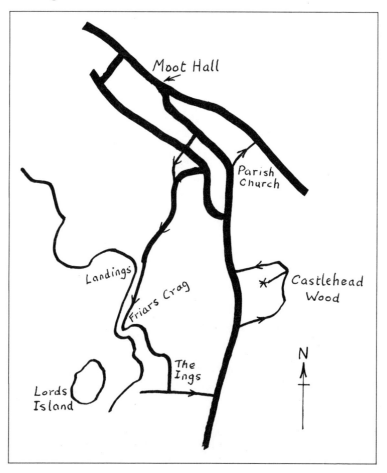

A further memorial will be seen only yards from Friar's Crag. This one is to John Ruskin and takes the form of a large upright slab of rock. Upon it, Ruskin recalls that the first event of consequence in his life was being taken by his nurse to the brow of the crag.

From this brow the isle to your left is Lord's Island backed by smaller Rampsholme Island with, to its right, Saint Herbert's Island. There are rocky outcrops between Friar's Crag and this latter, the haunt of cormorants.

Beyond the head of the lake and sandwiched in the Jaws of Borrowdale is the low yet precipitous Castle Crag.

Bill tells of standing at Friar's Crag on a quiet week day recording the view on his video camera. Tranquillity was rudely interrupted by the sounds of the lesser spotted crisp crackler, Homo Sapien, the noise of which came through loud and clear akin to the crackle of a machine gun. Not one to waste words, Bill quickly resolved this minor difficulty by finishing the crisps himself before continuing filming.

Notice a sunken fence to your left, head in this direction by gate giving access to a permissive path skirting the shingle shore. The time to be here is not midday but sunrise – sunrise, or just before, during late October, a still day, mist rising from the lake, the only sound that of lapping water. Looking into Strandshag Bay, on occasion a yacht moored here has only the mast showing until the sun gets to work dispersing the mist. A little later, as the sun climbs in the sky, Cat Bells will be bathed in its autumn glory – but you must be up early, the moment of magic is but fleeting and past its best in minutes. At times, clouds are piled upon the fells in such a way that down Borrowdale it appears there is yet another range beyond. More than once I have tried to identify these until the truth has dawned. No pun intended.

Follow the path to enter The Ings after crossing the fringe of a reed bed. This is very damp woodland being waterlogged most of the year and doubtless a rich breeding ground for wildlife. The route is however well maintained, so there is no danger of you growing webbed feet.

Pass through a gate at the southern end of the wood bearing left to cross a cattle grid before heading for the valley road running through the heart of Borrowdale. Reaching the road, turn left onto a footpath thankfully screened from this busy highway. A notice quotes the Highways Act 1835 Section 72 forbidding the passage of horses. It is conspicuously silent on mountain bikes, the rider of one having done his best to run me down.

Approach the 30 m.p.h. limit near a monstrous concrete lamp post. Cross the road to enter Castlehead Wood by kissing gate.

Initially the main path climbs straight ahead though soon meeting another. Here bear right to skirt the eastern fringes of the wood comprised mainly of birch; beech and oak with thickets of bramble. There are impressive crags on your left as a slight descent is encountered. This is a little disconcerting when in fact you wish to ascend. Patience. The track forks. Swing left on an easy grade. Where it meets a wider track follow this uphill, at a fence corner continuing ahead to gain the summit rocks of Castlehead Wood. The view is the more pleasing, hidden as it is until the last moment when approached as it were from the rear. On the last visit, the sun broke through as I scrambled up rocks to find two unoccupied bench seats. A super butty stop. In fact the wood is a microcosm of typical Lake District woodland.

Facing east the view of high ground commences with Clough Head followed by Walla Crag; Falcon Crags; King's How; Castle Crag; Glaramara; High Spy; Maiden Moor; Cat Bells just topped by Hindscarth; Robinson; with way back the Red Pike ridge; Ard Crags seen over Rowling End; Causey Pike and the Whinlatter Fells. Keswick is framed by a glorious Scots Pine, a photogenic location; Bassenthwaite Lake leading the eye to Dodd and the Skiddaw massif.

Return by same route to the fence corner, here turning left by a solitary bench, the view from which, towards St Johns Parish Church, has been overtaken by nature. Continue down the slope to emerge on the same road though only 150 yards from the roundabout on the outskirts of Keswick.

Walk against the traffic flow down the one way system which will return you to the Moot Hall. A detour is worthwhile to the right where a sign indicates "Public footpath to the lake 70 yards". Go by opposite direction into the churchyard of St John's to enjoy further grand views of Newlands Valley. Author High Walpole's (Herries Chronicles) grave is close by. "In loving memory 1844-1941, man of letters; lover of Cumberland; friend of his fellow men". A worthy epitaph.

From the far end of the churchyard turn left into St John Street to return to the Moot Hall.

Through Woods to Watendlath

Start: Borrowdale Hotel – Finish: Rosthwaite, Borrowdale. Grid ref. 261183. A linear walk of great beauty though initially over steep ground. Octogenarians should first either seek their G.P.s guidance or simply like some I know throw caution to the winds, step out and enjoy themselves. After ½ mile the walking becomes easy, the views stupendous. This walk is based on use of the valley bus service, alighting at the Borrowdale Hotel and returning – presumably to Keswick – by rejoining it at Rosthwaite.
Distance: 3½ miles.
Climbing: 900 feet.
Time: 2½ hours.
Map: English Lakes: 1:25000 North West.
Public Transport: C.M.S. route 79, the Borrowdale bus. (Note, no Sunday service out of season.)

Start:
FROM the Borrowdale Hotel retrace your steps to High Lodore Farm which offers refreshments. In fact the walk is singularly well provided in this respect, similar facilities being available at Watendlath and Rosthwaite.

A sign "Public footpath" indicates the track swinging to the rear of the farm where steep climbing commences. This is Ladder Brow, thoughtfully named – just keep putting one foot above the other. The woodland around here is predominately silver birch. Where the path forks, opt right, the left leading to a climbers' province seen through the screen of trees. Take it steady, this is a red mist job, or, as Bill puts it, "Sudden death". The track doubles back and forth until the gradient eases and, amidst acres of bracken, reaches the remains of a dry stone wall. From here the sounds of Watendlath Beck cascading towards Lodore Falls will be apparent. Follow the track, now descending towards the sounds, until in dramatic setting a rock pool fed by the beck will be found, sandwiched between Shepherd's Crag and Gowder Crag, a photogenic spot with Derwentwater framed in the gap.

Birch gives way to sessile oak as the path swings away from the beck to meet a post and wire fence bridged by step stile. Bear right through a defile. A great place for an ambush so look out, Mum and Dad. Silence pervades and, if it is autumn the wood will be alive with colour – 16th October to 5th November is the finest period.

15

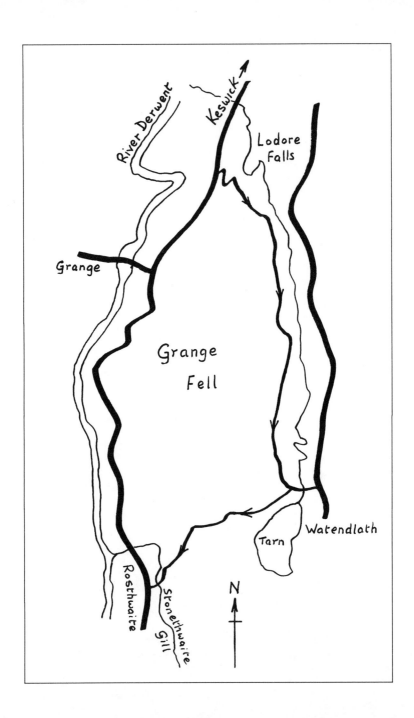

Move from the wood at a kissing gate, but do not cross the beck, following the track on the right hand bank. This is a most popular stretch having been both re-engineered and re-seeded in part with considerable success. Across the beck yet hidden from view is the two mile cul de sac extending to Watendlath, its presence detected by an occasional car roof behind the dry stone wall. Beyond lies the spine of the central fells. I do not use the word ridge as this infers sloping sides whereas the spine is in the main a wide plateau for which wellingtons are generally the most appropriate footwear.

From a recently erected long footbridge there is first glimpse of Watendlath, a hamlet of white buildings above a series of cascades. The path meanders up and down, flanked on the right by a mass of tumbled boulders, before a scramble over rocks brings the well known and scenic packhorse bridge under foot, this leading into the hamlet. A couple of ponies blocked my way recently near the bridge but only wished to make friends – probably after sugar lumps.

Sheep were about to be shepherded over the water, quite a crowd having gathered to witness one man and his dogs complete the gather prior to penning at adjacent Fold Head Farm which blazens its claim to be "Home of Judith Paris" the heroine of Walpole's Herries Chronicles. Caffle House supplies copious quantities of food and drink to be consumed with the willing help of the many tame birds which will visit your table.

The tarn is home to trout for which a licence to fish may be obtained in Keswick. There is a variegated selection of both duck and geese, likewise keen to be fed.

Leave Watendlath by recrossing the bridge. The path westward soon forks, the left heading for Dock Tarn which boasts a glorious display of waterlillies in season. Today, continue ahead climbing beside Bowdergate Gill . Spare a retrospective glance for the hamlet in its favoured situation sheltered from the worst of the elements.

To your left as you climb is Great Crag overlooking Dock Tarn. The path to both is abominably wet. Stay on your nice dry one, passing through a gate to the highlight of this walk through arcadia. Resist the temptation to fire off all your film, descending first to where birch makes a welcome reappearance. With these as foreground on the right day the glories of Upper Borrowdale will be before you. Rosthwaite lies at your feet, a sward leading the eye through Seathwaite to ranges of azure fells. This is a scene to sit and savour, always provided the weather is in accord. A haze of autumn mist mingling with the woodsmoke drifting up from Rosthwaite, the whole backlit by long powerful sunshafts into the valleys. During my last visit, a day of fast moving cloud, Great

Gable remained clear whilst across Styhead Lingmell and the Scafells lay enshrouded in mist. A backstopping situation for photographers.

Further down, at a gateway, there is opportunity for an optional return to the valley road via Frith Wood not far south of the famous Bowder Stone. Our course however eases left, eventually entering a walled lane on the left of which is a raised slab foot-bridge avoiding two minor fords which would otherwise be difficult to negotiate after heavy rain. The route becomes more constricted passing through rosehip; holly; blackberry and honeysuckle to enter Rosthwaite whilst noting that the Hazel Bank Hotel lays claim to be the home of Rogue Herries. Refreshments are available and hopefully the bus to return you to Keswick.

For those wishing to make a circular tour of this walk, it may be extended via Grange by crossing the River Derwent to return on the west bank, a further three miles if returning to point of departure though the last ¾ mile is unfortunately by road.

Through the Jaws of Borrowdale

Start: Grange in Borrowdale – Finish: Seatoller. Grid ref. 253175.
A linear walk initially through woodland, climbing beside a famous
landmark followed by traverse looking into the head of the valley
before descending to the hamlet of Seatoller. Easy walking. (Detour
to Castle Crag is a scramble.)
Distance: 3 miles (plus ½ for detour).
Climbing: 500 feet (plus 400 feet for detour).
Time: 1½ hours.
Map: English Lakes: 1:25000 North West.
Public Transport: C.M.S. route 79 Keswick-Seatoller, "the Borrow-
dale bus" alight Grange in Borrowdale.

Start:
GRANGE IN BORROWDALE stands aloof from the valley road
B5289 protected by single track bridge spanning the River Derwent.
Several establishments offer accomodation. Cafes thrive. Limited
parking only is available near the bridge. From here walk into the
village to turn left at the signpost, "Bridleway Honister Rosthwaite
and Seatoller".

Pass "The Cottage" where roses make a spectacular start to this
walk in season. Tarmac is underfoot through woodland, shading
a well-used pedestrian and vehicular route on the west side of
Borrowdale. The fell to your right is Maiden Moor from which my
wife and I made a dramatic and speedy descent to Peace How
through bracken and outcrop many years ago. She has never really
forgiven me for that day.

Soon the paths fork. Go left, skirting Dalt Wood. The area is
extremely popular with campers, which explains the wheeled traffic
which bounces along the now unsurfaced track. Stan and I came
this way recently to find, a couple of hundred yards further on
where the river flows close by, a family who had erected table,
chairs and parasol on a shingle bank in mid stream. Radio One
blared forth from a machine which would have swamped the
Albert Hall. Generally, better taste may be expected, no not
Radio Three, rather the music of nature, infinitely superior to
man's puny efforts.

Two streams require fording, though wooden walkways provide
a wet weather alternative. Having crossed the second take to a
clear path ascending right through the wood. This path has recently

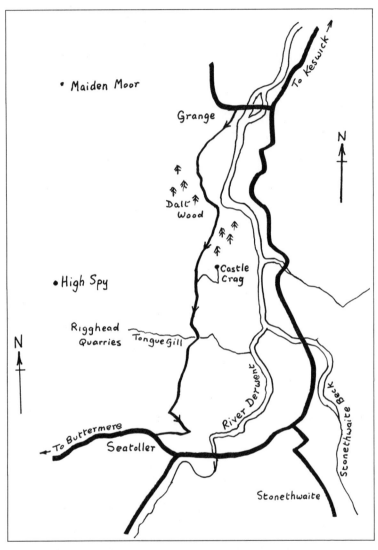

been re-engineered along with many others in the district, some at the instigation of the Lake District Special Planning Board, others by the National Trust, the largest landowner in Lakeland. At a gate, woodland gives way to fellside on the right. This is Low Scawdel over which towers aptly-named High Spy.

Broadslack Gill accompanies our route to a large cairn. At this point look back for a breathtaking view encompassing Derwentwater backed by Skiddaw and the Blencathra group, further east Walla Crag climbing to Bleaberry Fell. A good foreground is provided for photographers by a solitary hawthorn just beyond the cairn.

A decision will now have to be made – just when you were beginning to unwind and enjoy yourself too. The secondary track leads left to Castle Crag which has been building up aggressively on that flank. It is not even given a mention on the 1:25000 map, merely passing as "Old Quarries" south of High How Wood. Yet Wainright reckons the square mile centred on Castle Crag to be the most beautiful in Lakeland. If taking the detour to its summit, climb a wall beyond which a seat provides nearly the same view previously described. From there the track steepens, climbing heaps of spoil to emerge over the face of a long-disused quarry near the summit, itself a large slab of rock topped by substantial cairn. Castle Crag has the unique distinction of being the only summit under 1000 feet meriting a chapter to itself as described by Wainright in his seven Lakeland guides. Return by the same route.

Rejoining the main path, a col is quickly reached. Contrast the view behind with what lies ahead. From an easy terrace look down on fields patterned around Rosthwaite. Beyond, Greenup Gill climbs to High Raise though eclipsed from here by the dramatic face of Eagle Crag. Swinging east are Rosthwaite Fell; (Bessyboot) Glaramara; Great End and, leading to the latter the track via Esk Hause. The terrace is a former packhorse route serving old quarries, the spoil from which litters the fellside to your right. Paths still lead into some of them.

At a junction, take the lower, initially less distinct course descending to a footbridge spanning Tongue Gill. Just beyond, a further path joins from the higher route recently vacated and serving the former extensive Rigghead quarries near Dalehead Tarn.

Ignore a track descending to Johnny's Wood, continuing instead on the contour shortly to be joined by a wall on your left. From here, looking back yet again it will be seen just how dramatic is the situation of Castle Crag. At a small col, Great End will on a clear day dominate the skyline. Grains Gill (Ruddy Gill in its higher reaches due to the incidence of red ore) leading to Esk Hause bound for the Scafells. Grains Gill is described elsewhere in this book.

At a wall junction, pass through the left hand gate before descending to join the old road linking Borrowdale with Honister, this serving the quarries before the more recent motor road was built. Pass a belt of Scots pines and oaks before swinging right, down a well-graded gated track to enter Seatoller at the top of the village.

Refreshments are available in the village including at the information centre, Seatoller Barn which has a slightly incongruous air, approached as it is through a selection of farm machinery from yesteryear. The welcome, however, is heartening, John Wootton treating Stan and I to a resumé of the centre's activities. It lies on the course of Wainright's Coast to Coast walk, as such being a staging point for ravenous travellers. For this reason hot and cold beverages are available plus a plentiful supply of chocolate-based snacks much in demand for preventing "Bonk" on the fells.

Walk down to the car park where the happily named "Borrowdale Bus" makes regular journeys to Keswick. I am reliably informed that notwithstanding the glories of this route the driver also receives payment!

Styhead and Sprinkling Tarns

Start and Finish: Seathwaite in Borrowdale. Grid ref. 235122. A sortie into rugged mountain scenery in the heart of the district. Visiting two famous tarns in wild settings prior to returning by alternative route. This is the most arduous walk in the book, calling for good weather and stout footwear. The whole walk is however on well defined paths, there being no difficulty in route finding. Views are tremendous and as an introduction to the high fells it takes some beating.
Distance: 6½ miles.
Climbing: 2150 feet.
Time: 5 hours.
Map: English Lakes: 1:25000 North West. (A very small portion is on the south west sheet though so minute as to cause no problem.)
Public Transport: C.M.S. route 79 "the Borrowdale bus" runs from Keswick to Seatoller 1¼ miles from Seathwaite. In the absence of private transport, the extra distance may well take this walk out of the family category.

Start:
SEATHWAITE basks in the glory of being the wettest place in England. There will doubtless be other challengers though the rain gauges on Seathwaite Fell are the nearest to the hub of Lakeland centred on Great Gable, a renowned manufacturer of mucky clouds.

The Edmondson family of Seathwaite have achieved considerable fame with, until recently, four generations living in the cluster of buildings which make up the hamlet. There is a trout farm to the rear of the main complex of buildings, and on your return from a day on the high fells the cafe will provide fish to your preference.

To the west the impressive cascades of Sour Milk Gill tumble from the hanging valley of Gillercomb to swell the already considerable waters of Styhead and Grains Gills in forming the River Derwent. To the north of Sour Milk Gill are several spoil heaps, the remains of plumbago or wadd mines. The mining dates back to the reign of Elizabeth 1, the mineral being so valuable at the time that an armed escort was provided as it was transported from the valley.

Follow a clear path south, soon to be accompanied by the River Derwent though heading in the opposite direction. Several minor gills are crossed before, after threequarters of a mile, arriving at Stockley Bridge. Here an ancient packhorse route crosses the bridge to climb steeply on its journey to Wasdale. Below the bridge a deep blue pool is tempting in hot weather. Many simply sit and gaze at this place, further walking falling into the hard labour category.

As Bill and Stan (both grandads now) and I approached the bridge recently we met and passed a young family, mum carrying baby in a papoose, dad obviously suffering the effects of a recent accident, walking with considerable difficulty with the aid of sticks. His eyes though said it all, taking in the drama around. You do not need to walk vast distances or bear huge packs to appreciate the beauty of the Lake District. You do need to use your eyes and ears and give your mouth a rest. Bear this in mind as you toil up the steep section, through a gate breaching a drystone wall, before, nearing the 1000 foot contour, Taylorgill Force is glimpsed through a screen of larch and birch tumbling in tumult to meet Grains Gill near Stockley Bridge. Rowan and Scots pine are also in evidence though these will be the last trees seen until return to the valley.

Greenhow Knott is a good place for a breather looking down valley to King's How and, way in the distance, Blencathra. An alternative route hugs the far bank of the gill, but this has not been maintained as has ours by relaying of the path with the natural stone to hand, particularly on the steep sections. As we enjoyed a flask of tea, friends of Stan chanced by from Darlington where he once lived.

At Airy's Bridge the track crosses Styhead Gill to favour the western bank, following this to Styhead Tarn nestling in the lea of Great Gable and Great End. To the east the mass of Seathwaite Fell lives up to its reputation.

"Does it always rain here?" enquired a visitor of a local farmer.

"Nay, sometimes it snaws," came the laconic reply.

Seathwaite Fell proved for me the most difficult of all the Wainright peaks, three attempts being required before eventually gaining its summit. Twice I attempted to breach Aaron Crags from the north, a route if not exactly recommended then suggested by A.W. The rain sluiced down, entering my environs via upturned cagoul sleeves to depart, slightly warmed, seconds later via my "Waterproof" overtrousers. I would have been no wetter if I'd stood in Styhead Tarn. Third time lucky, by another route on a grand day, it was eventually conquered.

On a good day, there are many who will give up at Styhead Tarn, yet there is better to follow. Continue southward, still climbing, noting on your right the scree ravine of Aaron Slack forming a speedy descent from aptly named Windy Gap.

Soon, Styhead itself will be underfoot, a mountain rescue box dominating the scene. The story goes of a lost and weary walker on a foul evening chancing on the substantial box which stands clear of the ground. He climbed inside for shelter, eventually falling asleep. Awakening, the end door had blown to and he could not shift it. His cries were in turn heard by another distressed wayfarer looking for help. Releasing the first proved the salvation of the second, one assisting the other back to the valley and safety.

Styhead is a major crossroads. Viewed anticlockwise, paths lead up to the summit of Great Gable; around its traverse, the Gable Girdle; the regular route down to Wasdale Head; a more sporting

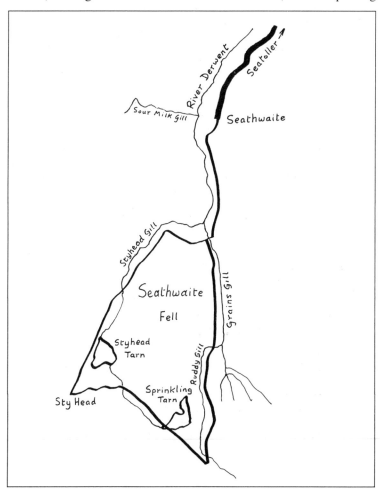

variety following Lingmell Beck; the corridor route bound for Lingmell col and finally our choice; the track bound for Esk Hause and the Scafells. Rumour has it there is a proposal to install traffic lights here shortly, which in the light of what follows may not be so facetious.

No sooner had we left Styhead than three mountain bikers sped into view descending the boulder strewn track at speed. We remarked on the skidmarks causing havoc to the surface, debating whether a bridleway is legally a cycleway.

Two thirds of a mile brings the second of the walks objectives into view; Sprinkling Tarn. This can be an ideal spot for a major butty stop. We rate butty stops – on a good day Sprinkling Tarn in the lee of rocks on its western bank would warrant at least three stars. On a bad one... The tarn is actually on a shelf forming the southern extremity of Seathwaite Fell, the summit being most easily gained from here. Other smaller tarns adorn its undulating ridge, the accepted summit being at it northern end. To your right is the tremendous face of Great End, highest peak in the district under 3000 feet. Its north face offers many ice climbs in winter though definitely not recommended for family walkers.

Continue with or without sustenance up the track to meet Ruddy Gill on your left beyond a rise. It is so named after the haematite which freely outcrops in this area. Here look left for a recently-engineered descent to cross the gill and enter the upper reaches of an initially constricted ravine through which Ruddy Gill thrashes and spumes in its headlong dash for Borrowdale.

The path here had in recent years become both widespread and dangerous. Now it has largely been relaid. Nevertheless it requires care, particularly in descent and after rain. Walking and gawping are uneasy companions so do not attempt both at once. Way below in mid Borrowdale is Castle Crag looking diminutive from this lofty stance. To its left High Spy and Maiden Moor; on its right Kings How and Glaramara, whilst in the far distance shimmers Derwentwater backed by Skiddaw and Blencathra.

A recent innovation is a hut on the left in descent and possibly used by the path improvers. Ruddy Gill is crossed by a substantial footbridge before gaining several feeders and becoming Grains Gill. A further half mile of descent brings return to Stockley Bridge from where the outward route is retraced to Seathwaite. You will have earned that fish dish and, if perchance the joints are getting a little rheumaticky a fish diet is worth a try. Its worked for me.

The Buttermere Round

Start and Finish: Buttermere village, grid reference 175170. An easy circuit of this deservedly popular, "lake" plus optional diversion from the south west shore. An excellent half day for those with small children. In summer, weekday and weekend alike, Buttermere is a honeypot for tourists. During the three remaining, and to my mind preferable seasons it is still possible to enjoy some tranquillity mid-week. There is pay parking adjacent the two hotels whilst "off street parking" extends way up the Newlands road at busy periods.
Distance: 4 miles.
Climbing: minimal.
Time: 2 hours.
Map: English Lakes: 1:25000 North West.
Public Transport: Mountain Goat service three times daily in season from Keswick.

Start:
BEFORE sallying forth, those of like mind may consider visiting the little church set by the junction of roads west of the hotels. Here, on November 3rd 1991 a plaque was dedicated to Alfred Wainright, fellwalker; writer and illustrator extraordinaire who many of us have cause to thank for an introduction to God's Country. The plaque set into an inclined window ledge is favoured by the sun streaming over Haystacks, his favourite fell and ultimate resting place. The old window glass is not "true", adding an air of mystique to the jagged outline as seen through it. The plaque reads:

PAUSE AND REMEMBER
ALFRED WAINRIGHT

FELLWALKER, GUIDE BOOK AUTHOR
AND ILLUSTRATOR
WHO LOVED THIS VALLEY

LIFT YOUR EYES TO HAYSTACKS
HIS FAVOURITE PLACE.
1907-1991

Right, let's start. Enter Syke Farm betwixt the Bridge Hotel and church by "Public Bridleway – Lakeshore Path". Pass the farm outbuildings to where a track bears right, leaving the bridleway above a rocky descent which requires care when wet – which is often. Pause and admire the spectacle of Sour Milk Gill cascading from Bleaberry Tarn in the shadow of Red Pike, the most westerly of the three prominent summits on the opposite skyline. An excellent ridge walk – not on today's itinerary – links Red Pike to High Stile and High Crag.

A further notice ensures you maintain the correct route, in fact if you get lost on this walk, give up, it's so simple. Move now into an oak wood where the path, compared to what it used to be, is well maintained encouraging users to stay on it rather than fanning out to form a scar several yards wide as at previous muddy points. A plethora of kissing gates cater almost exclusively for those deeply in love. Others, either past the first flush of youth or simply more at one with the scenery will presumably have to show both patience and restraint.

Seasoned walkers will recall just how bad many paths and tracks had become a few years ago. The National Trust and The Lake District Special Planning Board have to my mind tackled the problem both sympathetically and with an eye to the environment.

A rocky headland projects to the water's edge, seemingly barring further progress. Here a tunnel some yards long was engineered by the then owner of the land, ostensibly to keep his employees in work during a time of recession. At the far end is a greater variety of woodland. Holly and beech mingle with oak. Across the water High Crag towers dramatically skyward. Notice the rake leading from lower right to upper left. Our small walking group have been up Sheepbone Rake on several occasions, always having it to ourselves except for the ubiquitous sheep.

At yet another kissing gate, the waterside is regained at the crossing of Hassness Beck, the main drain for Buttermere Moss way above, a shingle beach flanked by glorious Scots pines, in turn framing the nose of Fleetwith Pike. This is a grand route of ascent, passing on the way the prominent white cross erected in memory of Fanny Mercer who fell to her death from this spot in 1887. This route is not recommended in descent as verified by Bill and I who did it in the midst of a summer thunderstorm with seemingly half the mountain sliding before us. Fleetwith Pike was Colin's last Wainright summit in 1992, when we all made a pilgrimage around the head of Warnscale via Green Crag to reach Haystacks. A sort of belated "thank you" to A.W. Fleetwith Pike is also known as Honister Crag, its drama heightened by the scoop-like depression known as Warnscale Bottom.

The clear track ascending between Haystacks and High Crag heads for Scarth Gap, the only easy route to Ennerdale from the eastern end of this valley. It is especially useful to those bunking at that most remote of youth hostels, Black Sail Hut. Our route has been engineered in places to avoid road walking until the last moment when the only option is to paddle. A sign at this point reiterates that the footpath is permissive only. Take to the road for a few brief minutes to arrive at Gatesgarth where a parking fee of £2 has recently come into force. Here there are more glorious pines. The circuit may with equal facility be accomplished from this point. Still on tarmac, cross Gatesgarth Beck turning right to gain the lakeside path at a notice, "Public Bridleway Buttermere/Ennerdale". A large slate collecting box for the Cockermouth Mountain Rescue Team is on the right.

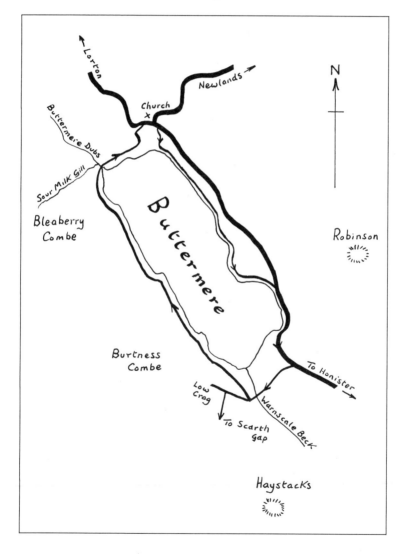

This path, previously a notorious quagmire, has been well surfaced apart from the immediate vicinity of Warnscale Beck where thigh length waders would still not be out of place on a bad day. There is a substantial bridge over the beck, the approach being the problem.

At yet another kissing gate (I must remember to count them next time) the direct route turns right for Buttermere. Here we will make a minor diversion, initially following the Scarth Gap path. Its course has been improved over recent years, the former scree track now being planted and fenced in an effort – apparently successful – to stabilize the fellside. Arriving at the crossroads by the fence corner, instead of turning left continue ahead on a less distinct track heading for Burtness Combe under the beetling buttress known as Low Crag. Here, set into a rock face, is a memorial tablet which reads:-

JOHN C. THOMSON
AGED 49 KILLED 15th JUNE 1969
AND
MICHAEL STEPHENSON
AGED 28 DIED 16th JUNE 1969
WHO GAVE THEIR LIVES IN
SERVICE FOR OTHERS DURING A
MOUNTAIN RESCUE PRACTICE

If you didn't put anything in the rescue collection box perhaps you ought to pop back and rectify matters.

It would be perfectly feasible to continue by this track into Burtness Combe provided you are suitably shod and the weather clear. A problem may occur in crossing Comb Beck if in spate. Once over this obstacle and a ruined wall, the climber's track from Buttermere will be gained for return to the village.

On this occasion, discretion being the better part of valour, retrace your steps 200 yards to the crossroads where you turn sharp left to regain the shore path. The large white property on the opposite shore is Hassness, a ramblers' holiday hostel. To the rear towers Robinson with right Hindscarth and Dalehead – a grand ridge walk from Newlands.

Crossing Comb Beck there is choice between the shore path and a bridleway. This time I'm opting for the latter just for a change – and because it's quieter. It heads into woodland, young oak right, conifers left. A little further where the wood turns stygian, bear left climbing slightly followed by gentle descent. Ignore a further track heading right. Larch becomes prominent creating a grey mist before the fells beyond. On a further rising grade a thin trod comes in surreptitiously from the left. This is the climbers' route from

Burtness Combe referred to earlier. At a tumbledown wall the track returns to the shore close by the outflow of Buttermere and entry of Sour Milk Gill, the latter crossed by minor footbridge. A larger one spans Buttermere Dubs, the feeder from Buttermere to Crummock Water. The path beyond has been much improved though still susceptible to the occasional overflow. Hostelries and cafe eagerly await your attention on return.

A Circuit of Crummock Water

Start and Finish: Lanthwaite National Trust car park, grid reference 149215. Mostly lowland walking though gaining height to the north of Buttermere village, before contouring the lower slopes of Whiteless Pike and Grasmoor thus avoiding return on the increasingly hectic motor road.
Distance: 8½ miles.
Climbing: 900 feet.
Time: 6 hours.
Map: English Lakes: 1:25000 North West.
Public Transport: Forget it. Alternatively start the walk at Buttermere to where the Mountain Goat bus runs three times daily in season from Keswick.

Start:
LET'S get the starting point right, it helps tremendously. From Lorton, pass the Scale Hill Hotel on your right, descending, note but ignore the sign, "Lanthwaite Green, Cinderhill Common". Below this and immediately before the crossing of Scale Hill Bridge bear left at "Public Bridleway Lanthwaite Wood" into a well-screened parking area on land owned by the National Trust. There is an honesty box for parking donations. Follow a good wide path into mixed woodland through which sunlight glints. Beech; oak and ash are much in evidence with good foliage undergrowth. Sheep are obviously excluded as the wood is regenerating itself. At a bifurcation take the right hand branch leading towards the lake's outflow, this being the start of the River Cocker surprisingly enough bound for Cockermouth.

Emerging from woodland onto the shoreline, Mellbreak should be clearly seen rising from the western shore backed by Red Pike; High Stile and High Crag. From the eastern shore Rannerdale Knotts shelters Buttermere village. A complicated selection of weirs and sluices control the outflow permitting the lake level to be artificially maintained to some degree as it supplies Workington and it environs. Stan recounted how he had read of a scheme proposed toward the end of the Victorian era by Lord Curwen to supply the greater part of what is now Cumbria with its water requirements. This involved quite simply, wait for it… damming Whinlatter. And we worry about the environment now! Common sense prevailed with the much diluted scheme now apparent before you. There are in fact two bridges at this point straddling a small island. Beyond, follow the lake's edge through an area of wild flowers, scabious and melancholy thistle being profuse. Cross a further bridge over Park Beck, the feeder from Loweswater at which outflow it is known as Dub Beck. Approach a circular structure enclosed within iron railings. This is the original pump house bearing a plaque commemorating its opening by Workington Corporation in 1903. At the termination of the low dam wall, stop for a moment to admire superb specimens of Scots pine to your right. A fence disappearing into the water leads the eye to a boathouse on the opposite shore and beyond via the cleft of Gasgale Gill to Whiteside and Grasmoor with further distant

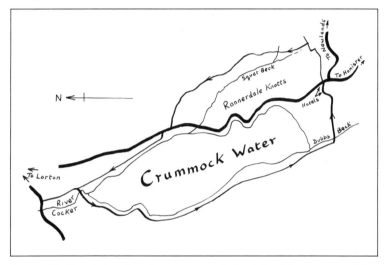

Hopegill Head leading in turn to Grisedale Pike overlooking Keswick. The Gill is an excellent route of descent – relatively easy on ancient legs.

Emerging onto meadowland the twin peaks of Mellbreak are on a clear day seen to advantage with the dramatic red mist ascent via Kirkstile End prominent. Swing west to where elderly oaks mingle with scree spilling from Mellbreak. The shoreline here is shingle leading to a wooden step stile. Cross this noting the range of lower fells surrounding unfrequented Loweswater, Burnbank Fell with its splendid terrace described elsewhere in this book descending to its western flank whilst Low Fell guards the east.

You will have to make a decision now. I know it's rotten and I'm sorry about it. It's a matter of conditions. There is a track at a higher level coming over from High Park which avoids some of the boggy stretches ahead. Stan and I prefer, when the lake level permits, to follow the shingle shoreline. The skull of a sheep on a rock outcrop leads one to suppose it had perished in the marsh.

Ahead the grand ring of fells enclosing Buttermere come into view with, from the left, Fleetwith Pike; Grey Knotts and Haystacks, the latter splitting Green and Great Gable. Natural oil seeps into the shingle from oozy ground above. Stan remarked this was all we needed, Texas in Lakeland with dozens of nodding donkeys to complement the hundreds of wind turbines seemingly destined for the more remote moors.

Low Ling Crag juts into the water backed by big brother High Ling Crag. Across the water a flight of late greylags cackled. We met the National Trust summer warden from Watendlath who entertained us for several minutes recounting tourists' reasons for not joining a body which owns and maintains a large part of the National Park for their benefit. In the heat a dead sheep hummed at the water's edge.

A crossing of Black Beck follows, the stepping stones being irregular. We found it better to take them in a rush rather than in a gingerly fashion but either way mishaps cannot be ruled out. Black Beck is fed by Scale Force, Lakeland's highest waterfall from which a path descends to meet ours near Scale Island – though not before negotiating a further leg of Black Beck which forms a sort of isthmus before entering Crummock Water. Beyond, the track has been improved with sections laid in stone where formerly was quagmire.

On the bank of Far Ruddy Beck under the birches is a good butty stop on the right day, mixed woodland spreading up the slope of Red Pike. The cuckoo is much in evidence in spring. Cross Buttermere Dubs at Scale Bridge before a low lying path leads to the village. This pasture is prone to flooding, indeed on occasion Buttermere and Crummock Water have been known to join forces. I have a series of photographs showing walkers struggling through three feet of water at this point, though this is exceptional. Now he tells us!

At a series of gates meet another track returning from a similar excursion around Buttermere, joining this to head for either one of the two hotels or the cafe. This is a Mecca for weary pilgrims and doubtless some of Wainright's ashes will find their way back here via the boots of the faithful on their return from Haystacks, his favourite fell and final resting place. I think he would like that.

On a previous sortie, Colin, Stan and I met a south countryman walking the Cumbrian Way heading for Carlisle. We escorted him from Scale Force to Buttermere where he was visibly overcome by the grandeur of scenery. Refreshment appeared to have a similar effect and was unlikely to improve his timetable, already way behind schedule.

Food is in plentiful supply at the inns. It amazes us just how many folk will tackle chilli on a blistering summer's day. Perhaps it has something to do with the name.

Pass left before the Bridge Hotel, crossing Sail Beck then immediately right into Ghyll Wood following the beck in ravine at this point. On a scorcher it is grand under the shade of oak leaves whilst in wet weather there is at least shelter. The first real climbing of the walk follows, not always welcome after a sojourn in the village. Through gaps in the trees Knott Rigg is in view whilst to the right the motor road climbs to Newlands Hause. Sail Beck which we are presently following climbs to its own col west of Knott Rigg beyond which Rigg Beck drains to Newlands Valley. A grand track through the mountains accompanies these two watercourses emerging near Rowling End rejoining the road.

Sessile oak which Stan, irreverant beggar, refers to as senile oak, is broken by stands of larch before our path emerges through a gate atop a wall at the edge of the wood. It is important (unless happy to end up in Keswick) to double back through a bracken-flanked track ignoring that continuing by the beck. Another path will shortly be met ascending from Crag Houses. Here turn sharp right at a rocky outcrop, a further guide if needed being a prominent juniper bush on the skyline. Stan thought it was hawthorn but declined to verify this so we shall never know. If you are interested climb up and find out, don't bother writing in, it's not crucial. Those who dallied in Buttermere will probably find this short climb surprisingly tough. Ignore doctor's advice and red mist, purposefully planting one foot above the other until a col is reached.

Stop here. No, I know you don't need a rest but I do and anyway it's a grand view. Across the valley Red Pike is seen behind its mirror image, Dodd, the latter being the false summit seen from the village. Eastward, Robinson reveals itself as a much greater mountain than envisaged from below, broken at mid height by Buttermere Moss, an extensive plateau. The Gables; Scarth Gap; High Crag and High Stile are all in grand array. Do you know Colin and I claim a world record for the ascent of High Crag via Burtness Combe? This we reckon to be the slowest ascent made, again on a summer scorcher – over 4½ hours. No claims please for bettering this, we will just take your word.

The Red Pike ridge is characterised by three combs, Burtness; Bleaberry and Ling. The 1:25000 ordnance sheet grants Burtness Combe an "E", Wainright doesn't. From the second which boasts its own tarn, emerges Sour Milk Gill, a spectacular cascade which tempts the ill-shod, ill-advised and just plain silly to attempt a scramble up its course. The patches of apparently dry moss which adorn it during periods of drought belie a treacherous wet layer only ¼ inch below, as evidenced by regular calls on the local Mountain Rescue Team to extricate those who have come to grief.

From the col take care to select the correct course, first left leading along the ridge of Rannerdale Knotts before making an excessively steep return to the water's edge at Buttermere Hause. That directly ahead tackles the unremitting ascent of Whiteless Pike, not on today's itinerary. Opt instead for the second left descending into the unsuspected side valley of Rannerdale. This was the Secret Valley of Nicholas Size, author and one time licensee of what is now the Bridge Hotel back in the village. The going is easy, soon following the course of Squat Beck. Before this is joined by Rowantree Beck look closely for a former sheeptrod heading right to contour the slope of Whiteless Pike on the 700 foot mark. You will probably miss it as we have done. Twice. Not to worry, in this event continue down the valley until meeting a junction of walls. Simply follow that to your right to rejoin the correct route. Although the trod is narrow, there is only one place after the crossing of Rannerdale Beck where any doubt may assail you. At a slightly wet section plunge fearlessly ahead to regain the trod on firmer ground.

Grasmoor End is now intimidatingly close, the haunt of, amongst others, the buzzard. Last visit we watched as one soared on thermals, two lazy flaps taking it out of sight around the end of Rannerdale Knotts. The bonus of this traverse is twofold, missing the traffic on the busy highway flanking the water whilst enjoying excellent views over Crummock Water and Loweswater. Descend easily to a wide path which in turn crosses a ford to meet the road.

After only 100 yards and possibly an ice cream van, escape through a kissing gate on the left into National Trust parkland – Fletcher Fields. It is as well to gain the shoreline directly to avoid a confrontation with prickly gorse, particularly so in shorts. Between here and the outflow is a favourite spot for the folk of West Cumbria, resembling St. Tropez on the right day. The major hazards likely to be encountered are push chairs; deck chairs and bikinis. Try not to trip over any of them, continuing into the shelter of woodland at a stepstile. Photographers may well at this point wonder whether a clockwise journey would not have been preferable, bikinis excepted, the opposite shore probably now being in shadow. The answer is to return and do it in the opposite direction. The route as described takes in the best of all available views.

Newly planted woodland follows before passing the boathouse seen earlier where a seat bears the inscription, "1889 MSW 1981". Not bad. Now the path becomes wider throwing off spurs both left and right which if ignored will return you to your transport to conclude a grand day's walk.

Loweswater by High and Low Road

Start and Finish: Fangs Brow, grid reference 106226. By high traverse along the slopes of Burnbank Fell and Carling Knott with excellent views up valley towards Crummock Water. Return is mainly via woodland on the shore of Loweswater. A walk for the discerning who prefer to be away from the tourists' honeypots.
Distance: 5½ miles.
Climbing: 500 feet.
Time: 3 hours.
Map: English Lakes: 1:25000 North West.
Public Transport: Nothing nearer than on the A5086 to the west of Mockerkin 1½ miles distant.

Start:
FANGS BROW is best approached by minor road east from Mockerkin, bearing right at Fangs Brow Farm to park 200 yards beyond opposite a gate bearing the notice "No vehicles beyond this point except for access. Dogs on lead please". It is signposted, "Bridleway Loweswater Old Corpse Road". A good track leads east into rolling rather than mountainous country. Left may be spied an attractive farmhouse. Gorse was still out on my last visit in mid November. Where the track swings right note but ignore a step stile to your left, this being on the return route via Hudson Place. The rising track has in the main a good base though stretches may become waterlogged after prolonged heavy rain. The slope of Burnbank Fell, a cornerstone of the group of five fells west of Crummock now lies ahead.

Pass through a gate with step stile to right, the reason I have recommended the walk in this direction now being apparent. Topping a rise where the accompanying wall stands back, a striking view takes in Whiteside; Grasmoor and Whiteless Pike. Right lies Mellbreak. Loweswater is partially in view backed by Darling Fell.

A possible waterlogged stretch may be avoided by detour to the right. Bracken is rampant and colourful in autumn. After a steady pull, approach and pass through a further gate. Beyond is a choice of paths, take the left, now descending and forsaking the wall which continues to scale the fell. A velvet sward is beneath your feet with Loweswater in a view which improves with every step. Kids will be in full flight down here.

The terrace is clearly engineered and covers the course of a pipeline to carry water from a dam across Holme Beck built by the

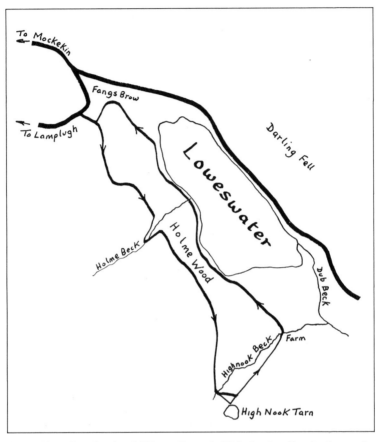

then West Cumberland Water Board. This beck effectively marks
the boundary between Burnbank and Blake Fells. The Mellbreak
foxhounds may well be heard in their kennels from this lofty stance.
Holme Wood is contoured by the terrace, its higher reaches being
coniferous, whilst beside the lake oaks grow in beauty and abundance, an area to relish on the return leg.

Swing right into a ravine breached by Holme Beck and spanned
by wooden bridge. The return leg meets the woodland boundary
almost exactly opposite where a track leads steeply down through
the wood to emerge at Watergate Farm, another spot to be visited
on our travels – but not yet. Notice how the trees lean with the
prevailing winds. My November sortie proved to be a trying day.
You know the sort. Hail; on with cag and overtrousers. Sun out; off
with them. Thunderclouds sweep over; replace them. Five minutes
later off again.

Retrospectively, during a clear spell I looked over the Solway towards Annan and the ugly cooling towers of a Scottish power station. Leaving the wood behind, a new foreground is presented in the shape of Black Crag, a ridge of Gavel Fell. Its aspect is forbidding, scree-ridden gullies tumbling to a small tarn unnamed on ordnance sheets, although Wainright has christened it High Nook Tarn after the beck into which it flows. The path descends easily, but notice before losing height the two prominent Loweswater fells, Hencomb and Mellbreak both seen end on from here. Each stands in splendid isolation, unusual in an area where ridges frequently connect a string of fells together.

Reaching the beck, cross it by wooden bridge, the tarn being hidden on a higher shelf. It is worth making a detour to this, lying as it does in a shallow hanging valley and appearing to have been dammed at some time.

Rejoin the path which in turn collects a former drove road. This has its origins at Whiteoak Moss before accompanying Whiteoak Beck downstream. Boggy country. Our route continues through a gate where there is good shelter in the lee of a wall and better view into the Vale of Lorton. A good butty stop. At the foot of Low Fell a prominent farmstead High Thrushbank lay framed in a rainbow during my November sortie. Cronky raven passed overhead. The high fells across the valley lay plastered in snow.

Pass through High Nook Farm, noting this is two words as opposed to Highnook Beck. An abundance of dogs will likely greet you from their homes on your left. Cross Highnook Beck by substantial bridge taking to a field path in 20 yards where a notice by a stepstile announces "Permissive footpath, Watergate". Watergate, that rings a bell. Not to worry, it is unlikely you will be impeached here. In fact midweek you will be lucky to meet anyone up to this point. Overhead powerlines offer guidance to following stiles on the same contour.

Enter the attractive environs of Watergate Farm flanking Loweswater. Beyond, in National Trust woodland, the lower end of the track descending from Holme Beck (and encountered earlier) will be met. Holme Wood is a most attractive place, its lower reaches being rich in ferns and flora and many ancient oaks. Shortly a bifurcation will be found. It matters little, my preference being right, passing Holme Wood Bothy, rudimentary accommodation at the water's edge where sweet chestnut stand in water at times of high tide. Birch is also plentiful along with the odd rogue conifer strayed from the higher slopes. Cross Holme Beck by wooden plank bridge. If followed upstream a spectacular waterfall will be found. Rejoin the main track coming in on your left. Pass through a gate into more open country though still hugging the shore, a notice on your left giving reassurance that you are still on a footpath. Enclosing walls lead to a gate and step stile. Now leave the water's edge, climbing steadily between walls where there can be quite a cascade after heavy rain.

Enter Hudson Place, a farm the first of three to be visited bearing the appendage "Place". A lion rests above a date stone 1741. Immaculate. Pass to the front on tarmac, in 30 yards taking to a bridleway marked Fangs Brow. Follow the wall on your left to a further step stile where an arrow gives direction. This section can be clarty, positively glutinous – cows! Trainers are not recommended. Gumboots are. Either way the kids will love it. Those of delicate constitution or car proud may follow the tarmac to meet a road climbing to Fangs Brow Farm so avoiding webbed feet. Those lovers of the good earthy pong of cow muck and not afraid of getting the car dirty – or better still travelling in someone else's – should pass through a heavily creosoted gate avoiding Jenkinson Place Farm by a track to its top side. There should be no difficulty in finding the third of the trio, Iredale Place Farm. Be sure to take the track left rather than entering the farm complex, a waymarking sign assists. Climbing now by metalled track glance back once more over Loweswater and into the Buttermere Valley whilst negotiating a gate. Ahead lies the Solway and Criffel. Notice a low covered reservoir over a wall to your left. Gone now is the typical lakeland scenery as, topping Fangs Brow the outward route is rejoined after scaling a final step stile. Bear right to return in a couple of minutes to your – or someone else's – transport.

Newlands and Littledale

Start and Finish: Newlands Church. Grid ref. 230194. An easy sortie into Newlands valley and the lower reach of Littledale, passing the former Goldscope Mine and climbing to an isolated reservoir in the lee of dramatic scenery before returning by easy path.
Distance: 3½ miles.
Climbing: 500 feet.
Time: 2½ hours.
Map: O.S. English Lakes: 1:25000 North West.
Public Transport: Mountain Goat Keswick/Buttermere seasonal only – alight Rigg Beck.

Start:
NEWLANDS CHURCH lies off the minor road linking Little Town, some five miles south west of Keswick and on the western flank of Catbells with the Braithwaite Buttermere road at Rigg Beck. Parking is just possible at selected points with care, notably where it crosses Newlands Beck at the foot of the hill from Little Town.

The church is approached by gated road at the entrance of which a sign reads, "Newlands Church ¼ mile". If it is more than 150 yards I shall be surprised but never mind, so often the reverse is the case especially at the end of a long day. Before dirtying boots, visit this fascinating place of worship still in regular use. In spring the carefully tended churchyard is a mass of daffodils. An extension to the church formed the valley school as recalled by a plaque "Newlands School. Built by Parishoners, 1877. Closed 1967. Dorothea Potts Headmistress 1943-1962". Inside the church is spick and span, boasting a balcony and two bells. Wordsworth wrote a poem about it, a copy of which may be seen in the vestry.

Outside is a parting of ways. Go left, noticing a meadow on that side free of herbicides. The mass of wild flowers are a joy throughout spring and much of summer. The farmer receives a grant to cultivate in this manner, not mowing until a much later date than is usual. The metalled lane is screened by oaks. Cross Scope Beck, beyond, again electing for the left hand lane.

Stan was leading this walk, Newlands being his favourite valley. Haytiming was in full swing with its distinctive fragrance as we entered the environs of Low Snab, T.V. aerial poised incongruously at the entrance. Well-tended gardens are a feature of the Newlands

Valley, this being no exception. Refreshments are available, indeed several thirsty and hungry walkers had already pulled into the pits and were refuelling a good half mile from base camp.

Leave by the southern exit of the farm noting on your right spoil heaps from the former Goldscope mine which dates back to the first Elizabethan era. A considerable gash in the fellside gives the clue to several adits – tunnels into the heart of the mountain. Never enter these even if tempted by gold. In fact the staple ores mined here were copper and lead. Silver and gold were a bonus. Don't waste your time going over the spoil heaps either, Stan and I have made a thorough job of it, regrettably without sight of a single nugget. Throughout Lakeland there are numerous similar disused and abandoned mines, the horizontal levels giving way to vertical shafts sometimes capped with by now rotten timber. You have been warned! At the height of operations during the 19th century over 2000 persons were employed in the industry within what is now the Lake District National Park.

The fell on your right with the dramatic ridge when seen from the church is Scope End, in itself a delightful climb to Hindscarth. Today however content yourself by contouring right on a fair track above the intake wall. Gaining the western flank, Robinson, a twin to Hindscarth is clearly in view, even having it own ridge, High Snab Bank. Between the two is the valley known as Scope Beck, strictly speaking Littledale being the hanging valley beyond the reservoir and still hidden from view.

Now on your left and at a higher level is further evidence of mining, a great chasm cleft from the fellside. The path passes two adits. At the second climb some twenty five feet to a higher track. That vacated simply follows an intake wall before petering out.

It appeared to Stan and I that this higher track might at some time past have been a watercut carrying supplies to or from the many mines.

Wheatear are in plentiful supply in the rough surroundings during spring and summer. If you look and listen carefully you may well see or hear a peregrine.

The track narrows, eventually disappearing in marshy ground. It reappears beyond only to split tantalizingly within yards. Take to the left aiming for two large rocks forty yards further. The dam wall should by now be in sight but first another wet section requires negotiation. Here Stan went in over his boots with that glorious sound reminiscent of a squeegee unblocking a drain.

The reservoir, built to supply a head of water to the various mines is in itself fed by Littledale Beck tumbling through a series of cascades from the higher valley, in turn feeding Scope Beck by an overflow of considerable width which in spate may prove difficult to ford. Stan and I pondered over this, he politely declining my suggestion to form a human bridge thus permitting my dry passage. You really learn who your friends are in such situations. Generally the crossing should not be too hazardous, youngsters will in any event be across in a twinkling. You can always walk round to the point of inflow where fording should be less of a problem.

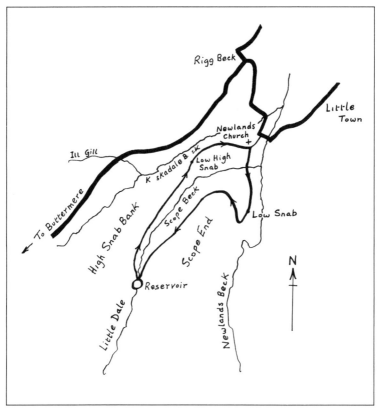

Safely over, bear right to gain a good path bound for Low High Snab. We put the world to rights for ten minutes, Stan having only recently moved to Lakeland to both live and work, telling of his daily lunchtime ritual walk to Friars Crag, Keswick, as he puts it, "Just to make sure it's still there". He meets and talks to all manner of folk on these constitutionals including a lady of eighty making, he suspected, a late pilgrimage to scenes of her youth before attending a school reunion at Wigton. She had travelled up from London (of course its up, you have only to look at the map) and was clearly moved at the sight of so much beauty just once more.

Meandering along the path, Stan pointed to a cluster of pigeon feathers, doubtless victim of a peregrine. I was reminded of a day earlier in the year when walking with a deerstalking friend. His keen eyes had picked out something amiss some distance off. Returning from the site, he instructed me to open a hand – into which was deposited head and feet of a white pigeon – still warm and all that remained of a peregrine's lunch.

Pass through a gate to enter Low High Snab. Beyond trees left you will glimpse High Snab and of course we visited Low Snab on the outward leg. As its name suggests Low High Snab is between the two, its title relating to relative position in the valley. Clematis and honeysuckle make a fine spectacle.

A tarmac lane now leads easily through woodland by lichen-covered walls back to Newlands Church to conclude this easy walk into a little frequented valley.

Outerside and Newlands Beck

Start and Finish: Braithwaite 2½ miles west of Keswick adjacent the A66. Grid ref. 232236. A very mixed walk, initially into mountain scenery to scale Outerside 1863 feet and overlooking Coledale, followed by swinging descent on an easy grade to contrasting terrain by Newlands Beck. Return by minor lane to Braithwaite.
Distance: 6½ miles.
Climbing: 1700 feet.
Time: 4½ hours.
Map: O.S. English Lakes: 1:25000 North West.
Public Transport: C.M.S. Keswick-Cockermouth route 34 (no Sunday service).

Start:
PARKING is at a premium in Braithwaite but is available off the Whinlatter road on the left some 300 yards beyond the village. Retrace steps to the minor road now on your right and bound for Coledale. Braithwaite Common is a usually peaceful haven interrupted on a last visit by a motorcyclist apparently intent on burning up as much grass and rubber in as short a time possible. Past the Coledale Inn is a seat inscribed in memory of Caleb Barnes the local schoolmaster for 26 years.

Swallows gathered in preparation for migration as Bill, Colin and I strolled up the tarmac passing a succession of cottages, one sporting a goodly supply of apples. Varieties of St John's wort grew in the hedgerows.

At a padlocked gate climb a step stile. Here tarmac finishes and the view ahead opens taking in Causey Pike as the dominant peak. Left is Barrow, an easy climb from Braithwaite and a fell we shall circumnavigate on this walk. Barrow Gill (a dramatic chasm 100 feet deep) defends the fell on this flank. To the right is Kinn, a level breather for those tackling Grisedale Pike and backed by oddly-named Hospital Plantation. This land was owned and planted by the Greenwich Hospital, London. A large remote property adjacent to the Whinlatter road became an isolation hospital. It has since seen service as a public house and is presently an hotel. Certainly this is an unusual site and name to find so far from the banks of the Thames.

Continue over another step stile to a clear grass path heading for Stile End. The main path swings to the left of this whilst a second

45

makes a frontal attack. Our course bears right a little sooner at a clearing in the bracken. Take care to pick the correct line climbing steadily to a tarn, Low Moss, between Stile End and Outerside. Here Bill located the musty scent of fox.

Look back over the vale of Keswick to the mass of Skiddaw, its satellite Dodd now practically shorn as though some phantom barber has gone berserk. This criticism apart, contrast the scene with that to your right on gaining the summit of Outerside after a short steep section beyond the tarn. Way below is Coledale, a metalled track leading straight as an arrow for Force Crag Mine worked for many years by McKechnie Brothers of Widnes who extracted barytes until 1966.

The once extensive mine complex lies idle though there are signs of exploration lower down the valley in the direction of Braithwaite. The National Trust now owns this land and have erected warning notices and secured all mine entrances. From a hanging valley quaintly named Pudding Beck cascades over Force Crag at Low Force.

Outerside is circumscribed by higher peaks yet is an excellent introduction to a range of grand fells offering a spectacular day's walking. From over your left shoulder when looking down on Force Crag the view encompasses Causey Pike; Scar Crags; Sail; Eel Crags; Coledale Hause; Hopegill Head; Grisedale Pike; Lords Seat; Barf; Bassenthwaite Lake and Skiddaw.

Between Scar Crags and Sail is Sail Pass to which climbs an initially clear path, becoming narrower and less well defined in the area of Long Crag, site of an old cobalt mine. In the days when we had real winters, Stan, young Michael and I had made an anti-clockwise circuit one January day via Grisedale Pike. It was crystal clear and very very cold. So much so I contracted frostbite whilst removing a glove to tackle a butty. Snow was crisp and care needed. Reaching Sail it became apparent that daylight was rapidly departing. A decision was taken to evacuate via Sail Pass to Braithwaite. Torches were reduced by intense cold to little more than a glimmer. Some 250 yards across the north facing slope at the site of the mine took fully forty minutes as ice steps were laboriously hacked.

Reaching with thankfulness the tarmac above Braithwaite we relaxed – and fell as one on our backs. Back in the car, torches, cameras and brains slowly regained usage after their dose of hypothermia. It was a lesson we never forgot.

Descend the south-west ridge of Outerside to a juicy though quickly negotiated depression to join the mine road below High Moss. This is a fast easy route heading for Stair accompanied on

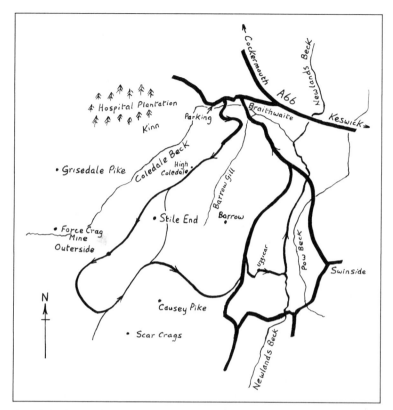

the right by Stonycroft Gill. Green pastures ahead are backed by two cats – Catbells and, way to the east, the pyramid of Catstycam.

The scent of heather lay heady in the September sun as we swung easily along until pulled up short by Colin requiring major surgery. A fly had trapped itself under an eyelid. Wearing contact lens, he was understandably wary of my opthalmic skills, though visibly impressed when the fly, after removal, took once more to the wing. More than that, he could still see and I had found a fresh vocation.

Beyond a circular sheepfold on the right, a path breaks away acutely to ford Stonycroft Gill before contouring Rowling End, eventually to meet the main valley road at Rowling End Farm. Our course continues to the left of the gill. Lost in vegetation between path and gill is the site of the former Stonycroft Mine, long defunct. Swinging north our path parallels the line of the Buttermere to Newlands road before descending to join it south of quaintly named Uzzicar, two farms reached by doubling back on a farm road to a gate through which a footpath is indicated. Do not enter the farmyard, instead taking to a walled lane bound initially for Low Uzzicar.

The nature of the walk changes here from one of rugged grandeur to pastoral beauty. Hawthorn and blackthorn line the route, which passes the lower farm to meet and cross Newlands Beck by a substantial stone bridge. Turn left to follow the beck, now canalised and flowing due north. Clearly there have been past problems with flooding, but now the raised banks form a haven of flora. This we decided was an excellent butty stop. In fact in the noon sun we all fell asleep, and I was awakened by a terrier licking my face. Well, it might have been worse. Two damsel flies went through their mid-air mating ritual – a rum way of carrying on. The tortoiseshell butterfly was in abundance though looking a little faded.

At a bend climb a step stile before continuing by the beck, with Swinside Hill to your right. A family of buzzard soared on thermals, mewing from time to time. The Swinside Inn will be seen at a road junction adjacent to the wood on rising ground. I recall an autumn morning whilst staying further up Newlands. Mist clothed the valley floor dispersing slowly when touched by the sun. As I watched, the inn slowly appeared above the line of demarcation floating in its silver sea backed by Blencathra. You have to be up early to capture such beauty. I have it preserved on slides.

At a second step stile it is just possible to make out the course of another though lesser watercourse, Pow Beck, only some fifty yards east at this point. Pow Beck drains the area between Swinside Hill and Hawse End. Despite almost joining Newlands Beck, by a quirk of topography it swings away to Portinscale as though to swell the River Derwent before, independent to the end, it flows into Bassenthwaite Lake at aptly named Rough Mire.

Our course follows the well-drained bank of Newlands Beck to the minor road bridging it on route from Swinside to Braithwaite. A simple ¾-mile stroll will now return you to the latter, passing well-maintained properties before crossing first Barrow Gill and then Coledale Beck. Refreshments are available in the village whilst you recall an unusually varied walk within such small compass.